PORSCHE

PORSCHE

David Vivian

Grange
BOOKS

Published by Grange Books
An Imprint of Grange Books Limited
The Grange
Grange Yard
London
SE1 3AG

Published 1993

ISBN 1-85627-253-2

Produced by
Bison Books Ltd
Kimbolton House
117A Fulham Road
London SW3 6RL

Printed in Hong Kong

PAGE 1: The sleek lines of the 1988 Porsche 959.

PAGES 2-3: The Porsche 911 Carrera 4.

THESE PAGES: Perhaps the greatest 911 of all, the classic Carrera RS of
1973. Not a car for the ham-fisted.

Contents

CHAPTER 1: The Porsche Family   6   CHAPTER 4: Toward 2000: After the 911   60

CHAPTER 2: 911: Triumph of Design   20

CHAPTER 3: A New Beginning   42   Index and Acknowledgments   71

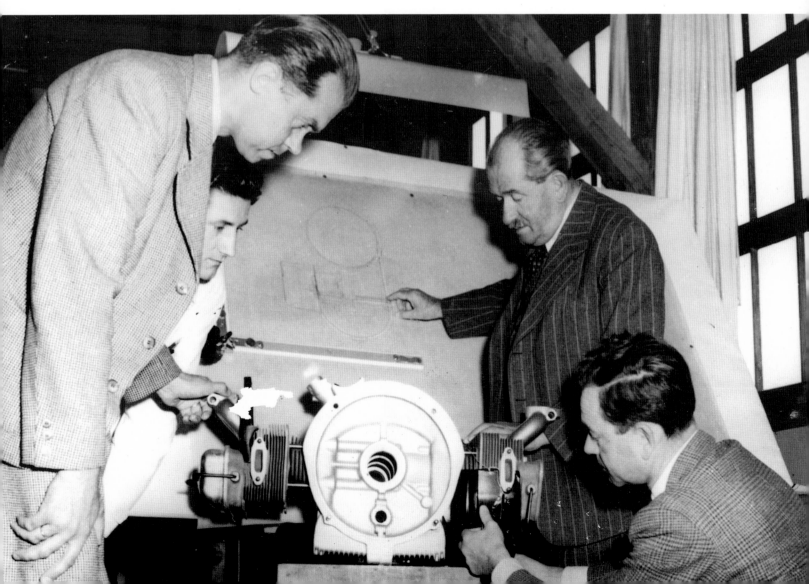

CHAPTER 1
The Porsche Family

Dr Ferdinand Porsche was born in 1875 in the Bohemian village of Maffersdorf where his father was the village tin-smith. His early career teamed him with Jacob Lohner in the production of an electric car before he was invited to join the Austrian branch of the German Daimler Company. This later became Austro-Daimler, where he oversaw the development of the Prince Henry model, in particular the aerodynamics of its bodywork. He improved the car's speed by reducing its air resistance with the famous 'tulip form' shape.

In 1923, Porsche joined Daimler in Stuttgart as Technical Director. He designed many successful models, none more impressive than the 250bhp SSKL. His instinct was to develop a smaller, lighter car, but this didn't fit in with Daimler's plans. So, in 1929, he returned to Austria and joined the Steyr group.

The timing could hardly have been worse, for in the following year the Bodenkreditanstalt bank collapsed and, among other small companies, took Steyr with it. But this merely precipitated the inevitable. With some money borrowed from German racing enthusiast Adolf Rosenberger, Porsche set up his own independent engineering design business in a small office in Stuttgart.

Porsche employed a team of 12 engineers, including son Ferry and old friends Karl Rabe and Erwin Komenda. Rabe worked with Porsche for many years, and was valued as much for his amicable Austrian outlook as for his first rate technical brain. Komenda was another stalwart, chief of body design and the man responsible for the Beetle's body and that of the 356. He was a modest and self-effacing man, but a progressive thinker.

The company was called 'Dr Ing hc Ferdinand Porsche GmbH.' Motorsport kept the company ticking over but its first milestone car was the VW Beetle, a car which provided the guiding principles for the first production Porsche, the 356. At the end of World War II, Dr Porsche – now over 70 and in poor health – was imprisoned by the French for nearly two years, but he survived the ordeal and, in 1948, rejoined his family in Stuttgart where son Ferry had re-kindled the family business and built a prototype that would become the 356.

He had this to say about his new project: 'From the beginning, we envisaged a small sportscar with which you could cover long distances without tiring the driver and co-driver. This idea couldn't be exploited because it didn't fit in with the national policy of the time. Three years after moving to Gmund in 1944, drawings were made for a sportscar based on the VW Beetle. The greatest part of our equipment had been lost in the war. Hardly any financial means were at hand, yet we were able to produce 50 high-quality cars in

ABOVE LEFT: Professor Porsche and his team with the first steel-bodied 356 outside the Zuffenhausen works in 1950. Steel-bodied cars went on sale in 1951.

LEFT: The air-cooled flat-four engine moves off the drawing board.

RIGHT: Wartime engineering involvement for Porsche.

the 12 months between 1948 and 1949. All were hand-made, reflecting the quality for which we were soon to become world renowned.'

The 356 was based on the design of a special aerodynamic coupe built around the VW chassis and mechanicals. Three were made to compete in the Berlin to Rome road race but the outbreak of war scuppered the event. After the war, Ferry Porsche and Karl Rabe adapted the design to make a mid-engined, two-seater roadster which performed encouragingly in trials. As the car was developed, Erwin Komenda styled a body, and the rear-engined 356 was born. It had an 1100cc flat-four engine developing just 44bhp, but was capable of 80mph thanks to its low weight and aerodynamic shape.

In 1953, Porsche the car was joined by Porsche the badge. What was to become one of the most distinctive emblems in motoring was designed by Max Hoffman, the sole US importer for Porsche during the Fifties and something of a marketing guru. Legend has it he sketched the basic design for the heraldic 'shield' on a napkin over lunch with Ferry Porsche in a New York restaurant. The final creation married the coats-of-arms of Baden-Wurttemberg and Stuttgart, and initially at least, was played down to such an extent that it wasn't placed on the outside at all and, on the inside, only in the center of the steering wheel boss.

Production of the 356 spanned 17 years, from 1948 to 1965. In that time, engine capacity climbed from 1.1 liters to 2.2 liters and power from 40bhp to the 130bhp of the Carrera. The basic design was straightforward – a steel floorpan with welded box-section sills and a central tunnel, not, of course, to house the propshaft, but for extra rigidity. The first 50 cars were hand-built but, when business moved back to Stuttgart in 1950, the need to boost the rate of production was solved by sub-contracting production of bodies to the firm Reutter Karosserie.

The 356's rear-mounted engine was essentially VW

Beetle by Porsche, the familiar flat-four design receiving cylinder head and carburation modifications from the engineers at Zuffenhausen, and driving to the rear wheels via a non-syncromesh VW four-speed gearbox. The independent suspension featured parallel trailing arms at the front and swing axles at the rear supported on flexible trailing arms. Transverse torsion bars provided the springing with telescopic dampers at the front and the lever-arm type at the back. Brakes were initially mechanically operated drums all round, but soon changed to hydraulic operation and eventually to all-wheel disks.

By 1951, 356 production had risen to 60 cars a month and the 1000th Porsche was made at the end of August. There were several minor bodywork changes but, more significantly, it was now made out of steel for ease of production. Also in '51, a bored-out 1300cc version of the original unit was introduced developing 44bhp but, later the same year, this was up-staged by a redesigned 1500cc unit with low-friction roller bearings, aluminum cylinder heads and larger Solex carburettors. Power leapt to 60bhp and top speed to

ABOVE: Gmund, 1948. 356 chassis number two is completed. Ferry Porsche (arms crossed) looks pleased.

LEFT: 356 production gets underway at the Reutter coachworks in Zuffenhausen.

ABOVE RIGHT AND RIGHT: Two views of the 1949 356, a ground-breaking design if ever there was.

96mph. Beefier brakes became part of the specification and telescopic shock absorbers replaced the lever-arm units at the back.

Changes for '52 included the introduction of a new, all-synchromesh transmission, a one-piece windshield, the addition of a rev counter, fuel gauge and clock to the facia, and the option of a radio. This was also the year the Hoffman-designed Porsche badge made its first appearance. All of this generated appropriate praise but couldn't divert attention from the handling which, at best, was being described by motoring writers as 'challenging' and, at worst, as 'very tricky', especially in the hands of the inexperienced driver.

The criticisms weren't lost on Porsche who, the following year, instructed salesmen to urge customers to become fully accustomed with their new cars over a few thousand miles before driving them hard. A positive Porsche initiative to improve the somewhat pendulous handling was still a few years away. Meanwhile, Porsche improved the refinement of the 356 with more soundproofing and a roller-bearing version of the 1300cc engine. In March 1954, total production rose to 5000.

This was the year the 70bhp 1500S was introduced. It had a top speed of 105mph and accelerated from rest to 60mph in around 10 seconds. The following year, Porsche started to make the 356 a better handling car by granting the front suspension an anti-roll bar.

ABOVE LEFT AND LEFT: The steel-bodied 356s for 1951 featured several minor bodywork changes but perhaps more significant was the bored out (1300cc) version of the boxer four developing 44bhp.

ABOVE RIGHT, RIGHT AND OVERLEAF: The 1955 356 Speedster was certainly the most glamorous of the breed and, today, is among the most sought-after.

The 356 evolved as the 356A in 1956 with further modifications to the engines, suspension and facia. A comprehensive redesign marked the launch of the 356B in 1960, and by 1962 smaller (15in) wheels, fatter tires and numerous chassis modifications had softened the ride and improved the handling. This year also saw the introduction of the 1600cc engine. More 'Bs' were sold than any other 356 – over 30,000 were built during its four-year production run.

A final version of the 356, the 'C', was unveiled halfway through 1963. Cosmetically, it was very similar to the 'B': tell-tale signs were the larger rear window and redesigned road wheels and hubcaps. The latter were necessary to accommodate the adoption of disk brakes on all four wheels, the icing on a dynamic cake now far more appetizing than that offered by the early cars. Engine options had been rationalized to two, 1600C and 1600SC, developments of the 1600S and Super 90.

The 356 reached the end of the road in 1965, 15 years and 76,000 cars on, a total built around a core of coupes but including the Carrera, Cabriolet and Speedster models. Today, any 356 is a sought after classic. Then, it established Porsche as a world-class player on the sportscar scene and made the company solvent enough to embark on its greatest adventure: the 911.

ABOVE LEFT: For 1956, the Speedster acquired a more muscular 1600S engine and a host of detail and cosmetic changes (LEFT) as well as modifications to suspension and facia (ABOVE).

RIGHT: The 1600S engine – more power and reliability.

OVERLEAF: The 356 Cabriolet differed from Speedster in several ways, including its deeper windshield and more sophisticated hood. This is a 1959 Super 90.

ABOVE: The 1960 356B embraced numerous modifications including new, higher bumpers with larger overriders.

LEFT: The 356 facias were the epitome of functionalism. A centrally-sited rev-counter remains as much a feature of today's Carrera models as the 1964 356 Carrera.

RIGHT: The crowning glory of the 356 series – the 1964 Carrera model.

CHAPTER 2
911: Triumph of Design

What red-blooded sportscar enthusiast hasn't wanted to own a 911? No one really believes that Porsche's most famous and long-lived model is the most accomplished sportster ever to wear a set of radials. It's the enigma of this unlikely, rear-engined VW Beetle descendant that people want to explore. Here's an uncompromising, wild spirit of a car, one who's fruit can't be plundered by the inept or insensitive but which rewards the skilled and patient so handsomely. It has, perhaps, the most loyal following of any car in the world.

In an object lesson to all other car makers, the 911 is made greater by the year, an achievement in itself. But when you consider the fact that its record stretches back nearly three decades, hitting motor racing (Le Mans) and technological (959) highs along the way, the feat is an extraordinary one. The 911 is small, agile, charismatic, eminently useable, hasn't an ounce of fat on it, boasts a wonderful competition pedigree, and is still highly influential without ever being fully matched.

The idea for the 911, according to Ferry Porsche, was hatched in the 1950s. 'As early as 1956,' he is reported to have

LEFT: The 911 – a legend among sportscars.

ABOVE RIGHT: Ferdinand Alexander Porsche – 'Butzi' – styled the 911's body; surely one of the most enduring designs in automotive history, its character shining through even in the 1986 Carrera (RIGHT).

said, 'we started with the plans for a new model. It was to be a comfortable touring car but, unlike the 356, parts from the large-series cars were not utilized as these were no longer suitable for further development. Various models were designed with a notchback with the aim of creating a true four-seater. But finally it remained a sportscar in concept, with 2+2 packaging. We didn't want to allow the Porsche shape, which had become world famous in the meantime, to disappear. As a power unit, a six-cylinder engine was chosen. But then it occured to me, remembering our motorsport activities, that front engines were not competitive enough on a long-term basis and so we kept to the rear engine.'

The successor to the 356 was powered by a two-liter, flat-

six engine developing 130bhp and made its international debut at the 1963 Frankfurt show. Porsche had wanted to call it the 901 but Peugeot was already using an '0' base numbering system for its models, so the new car was renamed 911. Dr Porsche's eldest son, Ferdinand 'Butzi' Porsche, styled the new body for Erwin Komenda to put into production – a shape that was to become one of the most enduring in motoring history – while Butzi's younger brother, Ferdinand Piech, designed the engine for Hans Tomala to develop.

To say that they got it right would be a gross understatement. Thirty years on, the 911 is still with us, faster and better than ever. And the trip has given us some great cars: the 911S; the Carreras; the lightweight RS models; the memorable Turbos ranging from the original three-liter car of 1975 to the current 3.6-liter Carerra 2-based car; the all conquering 935/78 racers, including the extraordinary 'Moby Dick' with its huge whale-tail bodywork; the popular targa-top and cabrio models; and the rarer 356-aping Speedster.

All through, the car has evolved – year by year, inch by meticulous inch. In 1969, the bodywork was made subtly wider to accommodate the bigger wheels and tires that went with growing power outputs. However, the first major facelift didn't come until 1974 when the bumpers were modified to meet new US safety regulations. This seemed as nothing, however, to the 'fat body' treatment accorded the Turbo the following year. With its massively distended rear wheelarches and tea-tray rear spoiler, some claimed the Turbo was a caricature, a 911 on steroids. That it looked purposeful and had tremendous road presence was beyond dispute.

ABOVE LEFT AND LEFT: Not all 911s breathed fire – this 1969 911E, for instance, pushed out a modest 140bhp. This was still enough for 130mph and vigorous acceleration though. By 1978, the 911SC (ABOVE) commanded 180bhp and 1982's SC (RIGHT), a formidable 204bhp.

OVERLEAF: The 911S was the first of the 'hot' 911s.

The 911 SC of 1978 had mildly flared rear arches – not as extreme as the Turbo's but wider than the regular 2.7-liter car's – less chrome and more color-keyed fittings. More for marketing than engineering, the 911 SC was re-named 'Carrera' again in 1982 and, at last, the range gained a Cabrio. A more fitting usage of the famous name came in 1988 with the Carrera 4, the most thorough re-working of the 911 since its inception, with smoother, cleaner styling for the 1990s, a new 3.6-liter version of the flat-six, 80 percent new mechanical components and, most radical of all, four-wheel drive. The rear-drive Carrera 2 followed soon after. Both were available with 'Tiptronic' whole drive line, a clutchless four-speed transmission with the option of fully-automatic or manual gear selection.

At this point, the 911 Turbo, Porsche's very own white-knuckle ride, had been dead for the best part of 16 months. That's where there the sober heads at Zuffenhausen might have left it if it hadn't been for the increasingly intense calls from Turbo die-hards to exhume the apocolyptically rapid, bad-handling old timer and thereby reinstate one of the world's most infamous supercars to its rightful place.

Never a company to ignore its customers, Porsche did just that. Moreover, the new 911 Turbo – thanks to a breathed on but 'green' version of the old car's 3.3-liter turbo engine – was even faster than its heart-stopping pre-decessor. *Autocar & Motor* recorded a top speed average of 167mph round Millbrook's fairly tight banked bowl (that's a certain 173mph on the flat). Even more impressive was the acceleration: aided by immense traction off the line and gearing that enables the Turbo to reach nearly 80mph in second gear, it scorched to 60mph in 4.7 seconds (that's half a second quicker than a Ferrari Testarossa) and 100mph in just 11.4 seconds. The drag strip benchmark standing quarter mile was despatched in a sizzling 13.3 seconds, with a terminal speed of 108mph. To put that into perspective, the old Turbo was good for about 160mph and 0-60 in five seconds.

TOP: The original 911 Turbo was also the most distinctive with its bold Martini livery. The 3-liter turbo engine delivered 260bhp and launched the 911 into the big time supercar league.

ABOVE: The Turbo didn't need fancy paintwork to grab attention – distended arches and whale tail spoiler saw to that.

LEFT: The 911 Cabriolet came surprisingly late in the production run.

RIGHT: Turbo or not turbo – be-winged or plain.

So was it more of that old black magic or the arrival of a new order? Unquestionably the latter. By using a modified Carrera 2 chassis, the new Turbo put its extra power (now 320bhp, giving a terrific power/weight ratio of 222bhp/ton) to far more telling use, re-drawing the sharp black and white division of power delivery with several shades of gray and erasing edge-of-the-seat handling for a genuine sense of composure, progressiveness and thrilling (rather than scary) entertainment.

The new Turbo cornered with greater neutrality than its predecessor, initial understeer gradually giving way to an attitude where neither end predominated. Lifting the throttle mid-bend still precipitated oversteer but, this time, of the benign and catchable variety; almost great fun. And with massive ventilated disks all round – 12.6in diameter front, 11.8in rear – plus advanced ABS, braking was little short of sensational.

The new Turbo was still a 911 at heart. Despite basically sound driving and great seats, general ergonomic prowess remained abysmal with a plethora of awkwardly sited micro-switches to confuse the newcomer, pedals that sprouted from the toeboard mushroom style, and supplementary instruments which were mostly obscured by the steering wheel.

The Tiptronic whole drive line became a similar subject of controversy, especially when used with the Carrera 4. In the eyes of some critics, an auto-drive line and all-wheel drive rendered the car inert and unchallenging, rather like a 'hot'

ABOVE: The 1987 911 Turbo Sport boasted an extra 30bhp and had styling overtones of flat-nose racers.

LEFT: For 1993, Turbo inherited a blown version of Carrera 2's 3.6-liter flat six, making it the fastest regular production Porsche yet.

RIGHT: The 911 Carrera Speedster, looking forward to the past.

pizza with all the chillis removed. Anyone who knows the 911, they argued, knows that it used to be the hottest, crispiest pizza in town. Its handling made your eyes water, its shift made you feel like you had five thumbs, its braking in the wet gave you the horrors. Only the brave or foolhardy ordered it and some wished they hadn't.

Porsche realized that, although some people will always

patronize the same old place, others would go off in search of tastier experiences. They did. Porsche had to do something about the menu. Out went the old 911, in came the Carrera: just as hot but easier to handle and no nasty side effects. More variety too: four-wheel drive, Tiptronic whole drive line, Turbo re-incarnation and, of course, the RS – all meat, no side salad.

Then came the Super Supreme: a normally-aspirated Carrera 2 with Turbo-spec wide-beamed body, suspension, wheels and tires, Cabrio soft-top and Tiptronic whole drive line. In other words a 911 in which you could see the stars, hear the engine, hug the curves and decide for yourself whether you want to be actively involved in the gearchanging process or leave it to a sportingly-inclined computer to do it for you so that you can concentrate on clipping the apex ever so gently.

In dazzling contrast, the lightweight Carrera RS of 1990 was the real deal, a 911 tough enough to satisfy the most demanding of Porsche die-hards. I drove it at Zolder and suddenly, inexplicably, felt like a 15-year-old schoolboy. It was an experience I recounted for *Autocar & Motor*; one I'll never forget. 'When I got back to the pits I was a bit out of breath but the man from Porsche was jumping up and down, saying that the French and Spanish had come back and that it was my turn to drive the RS. My stomach went

ABOVE LEFT AND LEFT: The Carrera 4, unveiled in 1988, was a landmark model for the 911, an essentially new car, at a stroke removing all of the question marks hanging over the old-timer's dynamic behavior.

ABOVE: The pure unsullied shape of the 1989 911 Carrera Speedster tail end.

RIGHT: Under the lid, the brawny flat-six has always looked deceptively modest.

LEFT: One-make racing has always been an important part of Porsche's competition history. This is the 1989 911 Carrera Cup model.

RIGHT: Turbo-styling with normally-aspirated mechanicals became an 911 option for the '90s.

BELOW: The popular Targa, with its removable roof panel, continued with the new Carrera models.

LEFT: The '93 Carrera 2, although the staple 911, is among the most powerful and fastest there's ever been – 250bhp, 160mph, 0-60mph in 5.1 seconds, 0-100mph in 12.7 seconds.

ABOVE: The Cabrio is slightly heavier but even more thrilling; perhaps the ultimate wind-in-the-hair experience.

tight and fluttery again but I gulped and said "all right".'

But it wasn't all right because another British journalist had got there before me and was roaring down the pit lane to do a thousand laps. Secretly, I was a bit relieved because I needed a few moments to tie my laces and gather my thoughts. Of course, I'd driven lots of Porsches before – 911 Turbo? No problem! – but I'd never driven round Zolder, Porsche hadn't brought many RSs with them and I didn't want to make a fool of myself (some chance!). Besides, I wanted to bone up about the RS so that I was fully prepared mentally.

There's not a lot to know about the RS, really. Like the old 2.7 and 3.0 RS Carreras of the '70s, this one's a sort of road racer with all the junk like electric windows, electric seats, folding rear seats, central locking, sound-dampening material, power steering and air conditioning chucked out to save weight. They've also ditched the regular steel front lid and fitted a light alloy one. The new front seats are brilliant – big leather buckets you can really sink into. They've even got slots in the side bolsters and backrest for a full harness. And this is really great. No door handles on the inside, just loops of some manmade fabric stuffed through a slot in the door panel. Hook your finger through the loop and pull and the door opens. Nice touch, boys.

Basically, what you end up with is a 3.6-liter Carrera 2 that weighs about 1200kg, which is about 10 percent lighter than normal. That would be neat enough by itself, but the RS is more powerful, too: an extra 10bhp makes 260bhp. Porsche reckons that if you're nifty with the five-speed transmission and know how much grief to give it off the line (what with all that weight over the rear wheels and a tightly screwed down limited slip differential, that means a lot, believe me) it'll get to just over 60mph in 5.3 seconds which is only a whisker slower than the latest Turbo.

Talking of which, the RS has the Turbo's terrific magnesium alloy wheels (7.5J×17in at the front, 9J×17in rear) and Yokohama tires with such a low profile they look like they're flat. Actually, they're 205/50 ZR 17s on the front and 255/40 ZR 17s on the back and you wouldn't want to pay for a new set. The body of the RS sits 40mm lower than standard and the suspension has stiffer springs and shock absorbers. The brakes are humungus: 322mm vented and cross-drilled disks from the Turbo. Otherwise, it's pretty much business as usual, including that titchy rear spoiler which sprouts up from the tail at 50 mph.

Not that there was much chance of it going down once I got behind the wheel. But when? I'd been listening to the

ABOVE AND RIGHT: The Carrera 2.7 – few cars could stay in touch long enough to discover what had just overtaken them. The situation hasn't changed much 20 years on.

LEFT: This was the real road-racer, though, the phenomenal lightweight Carrera RSR.

LEFT: The facia of the phenomenal 959 is virtually indistinguishable from that of ordinary 911s.

BELOW: The 959 has the same basic flat-six engine as the ordinary 911s, but twin sequential turbochargers boost power to 450bhp – good enough for 197mph and, with 4wd traction, ballistic acceleration.

ABOVE RIGHT AND RIGHT: The first 'ultra' car – Ferrari F40, McLaren F1 and Jaguar XJ220 all took their cue from the 959.

Doppler-shifted howl of RS after RS belting down the pit straight for hours. All the intestinal butterflies had flown away; I wanted a go. At long last, the Brit who pushed in front of me rolled to a standstill. Beads of sweat dripped off the end of his nose and strands of hair were plastered to his forehead but he looked smug and vaguely drunk. He fell out and I climbed in.

After a few minutes, Germans with brightly-colored spectacle frames were squinting through the window at me. I was so eager to get going, the two bits of the seat belt just wouldn't clasp together. Then, almost crying with frustration, they clicked. Clutch in, first gear, a bootful of throbbing, flat-six revs and I was away like a mustard-smothered frankfurter down a Bavarian's throat. Huge 'woof' from the engine, big push in the back, pits shrinking in the rear-view mirror, sonic kerbing to the port side. Yeah, this was more like it . . .

The circuit? I'd driven worse. The scariest part was turn one at the end of the 115mph pit straight. Go in too fast and you missed the apex completely, dive for the apex too soon and the tail would click out. On about my fifth lap – confidence hovering around the Senna-on-lap-of-honor level – I overcooked it in a BIG way. Suddenly, I was looking through the side window on maximum opposite lock, convinced that it was going to go right round. It swung back the other way but not so violently. What a battle! I had to take to the grass on the inside of the corner to finally straighten things out. The understeer-to-oblivion Carrera 4 wouldn't have snapped like that would it? But the old 2.7 RS would prob-

ably have had me in the tire wall. The new RS was just plain, bloody exciting. Grreat!

The best bits of Zolder were the up-hill straight between turn three and the chicane behind the pits (grab fourth before some serious braking and a little gratuitous weaving), the long left-hand downhill sweeper leading into the new chicane (third, flat, feel the neck strain), and the little left-right kink combination before the pit straight. Second gear, nice and easy, good for showing off to the photographer. It was the only bit that wasn't hard work.

Hard work? What am I talking about? In the RS, lapping Zolder was like a lifetime's worth of roller-coaster rides squeezed into a couple of hours. The new Carrera may not have had the explosive mid-range punch of the Turbo, but it compensated for that with instant throttle response, relentless urge and an exhaust note that gave me goose pimples for a week. The shift was short and snappy, the pedals heel and toe heaven, the brakes awesome and the stripped down simplicity of the package just perfect. Best of all though, was the way it handled. Grip, precision, control and, that old RS ingredient, *oversteer*. Porsche may have tamed the 911 with the Carrera 2 but they saved its soul for the RS.

LEFT AND BELOW LEFT: The 959's curvacious bodyshell was made from strong yet light aramid, a member of the Kevlar family – it clothed a galvanized steel monocoque.

RIGHT AND BELOW: The same but different, this is the 1984 Group B design study that spawned the 959.

CHAPTER 3
A New Beginning

Porsche's post-911 attack on the market was two-pronged and front-engined, teaming up the old-timer with a new entry-level model and flagship: the 924 and 928. In many ways, the 924 had more significance as a marketing concept than as a car. It was to be the first genuinely 'affordable' Porsche since the 356, a car with mass-market components yet one that would hold a special appeal for enthusiasts. A Porsche without driver appeal, after all, would hardly have been worthy of the badge. In the name of cost-effectiveness and to take advantage of existing well-forged commercial links, Porsche selected its key parts from the VW-Audi store shelves, the engine and suspension being just the starting point.

Planning started in 1972. A number of layout options were considered but, in the end, for the most even weight distribution and best traction, a rear-mounted drive line was chosen. Also, because the weight masses were concentrated at either end of the car, like a dumbell, slides at the limit of adhesion were more progressive and easier to control. This transaxle configuration, of course, became the signature of all new front-engined Porsches.

Skeptical observers, though, were inclined not to see a real Porsche when they looked at the 924, but merely an up-market Audi. They had a point, too. Engine and transaxle were from the Audi 100 and made by VW. This was not because they were necessarily the best components for the job, but because it was commercially expedient to use them, a consideration which fitted in well with the marketing strategy.

The engine was extensively developed from a four-cylinder unit that had been introduced in 1965. It acquired an overhead camshaft and a bore enlarged from 84 to 86.5mm which, with the 84.4mm stroke, increased the overall capacity to 1984cc. In time, this unit also ended up in the VW LT van. It made its debut in the Audi 100 in 1977.

What the engine lacked in breeding, however, it made up for in brawn. With a higher, 9.3:1, compression ratio and Bosche K-Jetronic fuel injection, the engine delivered a punchy 125bhp (DIN) at 5800rpm and 121.4lb ft of torque at 3500rpm. Larger main bearings and a forged steel crankshaft were additional 924 niceties, as was a special die-cast sump since, for the Porsche application, the engine would be canted over to keep the 924's hood line low.

Adapting the Audi engine proved relatively straightforward; not so designing a transaxle. It was a problem Alfa Romeo had already faced with the Alfetta, so Porsche bought one to have a look. On the whole, Porsche's engineers concluded that Alfa hadn't done a bad job. The one thing they hadn't been able to achieve, however, was a decent shift because of the long linkage needed and the

ABOVE LEFT AND LEFT: The front-engined, water-cooled 928 and 924 (above and below, respectively) were the cars Porsche thought would kill the 911. They were wrong.

RIGHT: This picture clearly shows the 924's transaxle layout – adopted, principally, for better weight distribution and traction.

LEFT, RIGHT AND BELOW: Racing was used to improve 924's 'rich man's Audi' image, mostly through one-make series. This is the 1978 AFN works car.

inertia of the revolving propshaft when the clutch was engaged – the latter making life especially hard for the syncromesh.

Porsche's solution was a 3.3in diameter length of metal tubing bolted to the engine and the transaxle that encased the propeller shaft, itself supported on four sealed-for-life bearings. This allowed both the diameter and the mass of the shaft to be reduced. The tube solution allowed the complete drive unit to be treated as one assembly, which made installation much easier. The reason it improved the shift was because the rigid tube made an excellent mounting for the shift rod which was passed through it, improving the quality of the shift no end. The new structure also acted as a support for the exhaust system. With these developments, the transaxle could handle a surprising amount of torque, a feature that would be thoroughly exploited as the model evolved. But there were drawbacks: the transaxle needed a big drive line hump in the cabin and stole trunk space.

No less of an exercise in re-cycling Audi/VW parts, the 924's chassis mixed and matched from the VW parts bin: MacPherson struts were from the VW Golf but with the strengthened lower arms from the Scirocco. Other Golf hand-me-downs were the rack and pinion steering and safety column. For the rear suspension, Porsche delved even deeper into VW's past, implementing Beetle parts with semi-trailing arms and torsion bars.

More basic still, the drive shafts started life in VW's 181 all-terrain vehicle, while brakes were Servo-assisted front disks and rear drums from the VW K70. Like the Golf which donated its coil sprung MacPherson strut front suspension to the 924, the Porsche boasted outboard scrub radius geometry, giving a degree of automatic steering correction after a tire blow-out or when braking on uneven grip surfaces. More typical of the Zuffenhausen brand, though, was the 924's sleek and very pretty body. Fresh, eye-catching details abounded – not least the wrap-around tailgate glass, integrated plastic bumpers and pop-up headlamps.

An honest two-plus-two and nothing more, the 924's cramped rear seats were only really suitable for children. Treated as a two-seater it made a lot more sense as, when the back seats were not in use, the top half of the rear backrest could be folded down to extend the depth of the luggage platform.

The rounded, soft-edged facia – Porsche pre-empted the curvy, 'organic look' trend by a good decade here – contained two instrument packs: a main display in front of the driver and, somewhat harder to read at a glance, a supplementary set (oil pressure, oil temperature and a clock) down on the center console. The rest of the cabin looked functional but a little austere. Production started in 1976 in the old NSU plant at Neckarsulm, initially running at between 80 and 100 cars a day. Just over a year later, a five-speed

transmission derived from that of the 911, with more closely spaced intermediate ratios, was introduced.

Engine power and torque stayed the same so it was no surprise that, when *Autocar* tested a Lux five-speed in August 1978, it recorded no jump in performance but did comment that it felt 'more lively and responsive' to drive. Both cars reached 60mph in around 9.5 seconds and 100mph in just under 30 seconds. With a top speed of around 125mph, the baby Porsche, despite its mongrel bloodline, was clearly no rubber-legged puppy.

Just a few months away, however, was a 924 with a bite worse than its bark: the Turbo. The 1984cc displacement remained the same, as did the whole of the bottom end which was deemed man enough for the job. All new was the cylinder head (aluminum as before) which used different combustion chambers, recessed valves, 3mm exhaust valves, spark plugs with the silver electrodes moved across to the intake side, and a compression ratio dropped from 9.3 to 7.5 to 1.

Blowing up the extra energy, the German-made KKK turbocharger drew air from the Bosch K-Jetronic flap valve box and air filter assembly mounted transversely across the front of the engine. A wastegate with blow-off valve limited boost pressure. The higher operating temperatures were fielded by an oil cooler and additional cooling vents in the nose of the car. The Turbo weighed about 220lbs more than the normally aspirated 924 but it had 36 percent more power (170 versus 125bhp) and a whopping 48 percent increase in

LEFT: Turbocharging also did the 924's image a lot of good, pushing power up from 125 to 170bhp. Now it had the performance to exploit its excellent chassis.

ABOVE RIGHT AND RIGHT: The Carrera GT took things a stage further. Visually, at least, this car was the forerunner of the 944.

peak torque, taking the figure to 181lb ft at 3500rpm. Transmission ratios and spring/shock absorber rates were altered to suit and there were servo-assisted ventilated disks all round. For the British market, the Turbo was sold with 205/55 Pirelli P7s on 16in alloy rims as standard.

As tested by *Motor* magazine in 1980, the 924 Turbo achieved a top speed of 140mph, 0-60mph in 7.0 seconds and 0-100mph in 17.9 seconds – cracking figures then and still impressive today, though the Turbo's long gearing and lack of turbo boost at low revs meant that those who weren't prepared to make an effort with the transmission wouldn't get the best from the car.

The 924 was destined to go still faster as a road car in the form of the Carrera GT. This was effectively the 'homologation special' version of the Turbo and, on the track, finished a remarkable 6th, 12th and 13th in the 1980 Le Mans 24 Hours. Some 400 Carreras were built to qualify for Group B. They could be distinguished by their Turbo-style rear spoiler and nose/flank body extensions made of polyurethane. A modified nose section cut the Cd to a (then) very respectable 0.34 while the more bulbous wheelarches

were needed to accommodate the 215/60 VR15 Pirelli P7s on 7J rims.

In essence, the Carrera used the same engine as the Turbo, but with an intercooler to reduce the temperature of the intake air. This, in turn, allowed the compression ratio to be raised from 7.5 to 8.5:1 and boosted pressure from 0.65 to 0.75bar, raising power by 33bhp to 210bhp (DIN) at 6000rpm and peak torque from 181 to 203lb ft at 3500rpm. Now 0-60mph was achieved in 6.5 seconds and 100mph in 16.7 seconds; respectively 0.5 and 1.2 seconds better than the regular Turbo.

Meanwhile, for the 1981 model year, the Turbo's KKK turbocharger was replaced by a smaller unit with faster turbine spin-up and, therefore, less lag and better response at low revs. In league with this, the former breakerless ignition was replaced by a Siemens-Hartig digital system which permitted the compression ratio to be raised from 7.5 to 8.5:1 and peak power to jump by 7bhp to 177bhp. This was undeniably the most exciting road-going 924 of all.

The last 924, however, was the 924S of 1985. Initially powered by a de-tuned version of the Porsche-made 'balan-

RIGHT AND BELOW: The 924S soldiered on alongside the 944, whose original 2.5-liter Porsche-designed slant four engine it shared. Note the up-market 'phone-dial' alloy wheels and tailgate spoiler. The 'S' was the last 924 model.

LEFT: The 928 – a big car with genuine supercar status, truly a new beginning for Porsche.

RIGHT: The 928's all-alloy 4-liter V8 was compact, light and powerful.

cer-shaft' 2.5-liter engine from the 944, it acquired the full-tune 160bhp unit and power steering as standard in 1987 and, with it, the kind of performance that plugged the gap left by the now defunct Turbo: 137mph, 0-60mph in 7.4 seconds and 0-100mph in 20.1 seconds. In truth, the big engine helped a fast-fading model to hang on for a few more months while the car it was always meant to power, the 944, found its feet. We'll come to the 944 later in this chapter.

The car that really posted Porsche's intentions in the late seventies, though, was its new flagship, the 928. This, the company confidently predicted, was the shape of supercars to come - a tacit acknowledgment, if ever there was one, that the 911 had passed its sell-by date. Porsche, however, hadn't reckoned with the die-hard fanaticism of 911 lovers. For them, the 928 looked like a betrayal of all they held dear. How, they asked, could a front engine/transaxle layout (the stuff of 924s for goodness sake!) ever substitute for having the engine over the rear wheels? And could there be two

more disparate engines than the 928's water-cooled V8 and the 911's air-cooled flat-six?

Porsche's argument was that the world was changing and that if it was to survive as a car maker, it must change, too. The 928 was the politically correct Porsche to ensure that survival – a car of huge ability and great potential, one more in tune with future legislation and more likely to broaden Porsche's market appeal. So impressed was the world's motoring Press with the 928 that it became the International Car of The Year the year after its launch at the 1977 Geneva Motor Show.

Work on the 928 had started six years earlier, instigated as much as anything by what was perceived to be the 911's increasing length of tooth. Porsche designed its 2+2 GT – something that would inevitably lock horns with the Aston Martin V8 and the Jaguar XJ-S – from scratch. It was to be a pure Porsche to the core: nothing borrowed from anyone else's parts bin. Its major design tenets, on the other hand, were precisely the same as the 924's: a front engine driving rear wheels with the transmission (five-speed manual or three-speed auto) rear mounted in-unit with the final drive to achieve, as near as possible, a 50/50 weight distribution. As for the engine, initial trials with a V6 (which would be compact and fuel efficient) were shelved in favor of a large, all-alloy V8 – a unit that would meet its performance targets without undue stress and, of course, be welcomed in the important US market.

More of a coincidence was that the 928's radically bulbous styling came from the drawing board of American Tony Lapine, then Porsche's head of design. Among Lapine's more memorable innovations were the large, deformable body-color panels at the front and rear, and the front-hinged pop-up headlights which laid back into the fender when retracted, rather like those of a Lamborghini Miura. Equally striking was the 928's proportioning. At 14ft 7in long, it was just 9in longer than the 911 but this just made its width of just over six feet seem all the more startling.

Clearly a shape Porsche wanted to be around for a long time, the 928 had corrosion resistant aluminum wheels, doors, hood, transaxle housing, suspension components, cylinder heads, block and crankcase. The rest of the car was made either from galvanized steel or plastic. It looked a heavy car and was, tipping the scales at a hefty 3200lbs, but it was a powerful one, too. Its eight Bosch K-Jetronic cylinders and 4474cc delivered 240bhp at 5500rpm and 257lb ft of torque at 3600rpm. A single overhead camshaft per cylinder bank operated in-line valves via hydraulic valve lifters and steel-coated aluminum pistons running directly in the aluminum cylinder bores.

Self-adjusting valves and contactless ignition, a long-life battery and oversized fuel and oil filters for the engine formed the basis of a minimum servicing regime, stretching oil-change intervals to a virtually unheard of 12,500 miles.

Taken at face value, there was nothing particularly 'cutting-edge' about the 928's chassis – just good ol' wishbones and coils front and rear, rack and pinion steering, and all-disk braking. It was the implementation of the hardwear that made all the difference: negative scrub radius geometry at the front for more stable braking when the car straddled surfaces with unequal grip; speed sensitive power

ABOVE: Porsche's famous 'phone-dial' alloy wheels made their debut on the 928.

LEFT: The rear and front of the 928 were made from a special deformable plastic – no visible bumpers.

ABOVE RIGHT AND RIGHT: American Tony Lapine was responsible for 928's uniquely bulbous shape. The glass tailgate revealed modest but nonetheless useable luggage area.

OVERLEAF: The 1982 928S, first of the 'hot' 928s.

assistance for the steering with weighting that became meatier the faster you went; and, most significant of all, the 'Weissach' rear axle (named after Porsche's R&D center) which had built into it a degree of 'compliance steer' that prevented the rear wheels from toeing out under deceleration or braking. This virtually eliminated lift-off oversteer. Tires and wheels were 225/50 section Pirelli P7s on 16×7J cast alloy rims, the brakes comprised large ventilated disks all round gripped by floating calipers. Twin, diagonally-split circuits and servo assistance were also part of the specification, but ABS wouldn't come for a few years.

The 928 was an effortlessly rapid machine, as Porsche intended, but by no means 911-quick. It took around seven seconds to accelerate to 60mph and just under 18 to reach 100mph – not hanging around, but Jaguar's XJS was quicker. Neither was the 140mph top speed quite up to the Jaguar, Aston Martin or Ferrari mark. What the 928 lacked in neck-snapping performance, however, it made up for in smoothness and lack of temperament. It wasn't too thirsty, either, with an overall return of around 15mpg. Rival Jaguars and Astons would have been lucky to better 11mpg.

Where the 928 clearly broke new ground for a big car was in the way it handled. Its steering set new standards of feel for a power-assisted set up, a virtue put to good use by the tenacious grip of the fat Pirelli P7s and the chassis' simply fabulous cornering balance with its broad neutral phase and final, benign oversteer. Tremendous straight line stability and immensely powerful brakes were the other big guns in the 928's dynamic armory but a lumpy low-speed ride was the unfortunate corollary of all this unexpected agility.

If the baby 924 was a token 2+2, the 928's pretence to carrying four people was only marginally more convincing. Despite its bulk, the back seats were for midgets or small children only, even though the front seats had enough legroom for a modest giant. As a two-seater, the 928 was wonderfully roomy and, as with the 924, folding forward the individual backrests of the rear seats gave a decent amount of luggage space behind the glass tailgate.

First and last, though, the 928 aimed to please its driver. Not only was the seat extremely comfortable, its basic relationship to the rest of the major controls ensured an almost flawless driving position. In an ergonomic coup that has yet to be bettered, Porsche fixed the relationship between the three-spoke, leather rimmed steering wheel, the instrument pod, and its attendant switchgear. Adjust the rake of the steering wheel and the whole steering column and instrument binnacle moved with it as a single unit, and what instruments – not just comprehensive but an object lesson in presentational clarity.

After the awkward crudeness of the 911's heating and ventilation, the 928's efficient, easily-regulated system was a revelation and the optional air conditioning was better still. Standard equipment included a stereo radio/cassette, cruise control, electric windows and door mirrors, alloy wheels and power-assisted steering. True to Porsche's deserved reputation, the 928 was beautifully built and finished.

In 1980, the 928 acquired the 'S' suffix. With it went a larger (4.7-liter) engine, more power, cosmetic changes

ABOVE: The 928's wrap-around facia and wonderfully clear instruments still haven't been significantly bettered.

ABOVE RIGHT AND FAR RIGHT: The 928S4 featured revised rear-end styling with bigger tail lights and spoiler, and disk-type alloy wheels.

RIGHT: The 1989 928S in a familiar 'bug-eyed' lights-up pose. Headlights retract backward, shark-like, when not in use.

(basically front and rear spoilers), and a fuller specification. The easiest way to spot the new model, was by its flat disk style 16in alloy wheels wearing the 225/50 section P7s of the original car (which, in turn, had its rubber down-graded to 215/60 P6s). Changes inside included a thermostatically controlled heating and air-conditioning system; a four-spoke steering wheel; and electrically powered seats with height, reach and backrest adjustment as standard.

As well as the hike in capacity – from 4474cc to 4664cc, the compression ratio was raised from 8.5:1 to 10.0:1, requiring the use of four-star instead of two-star petrol. Re-profiled camshafts and numerous smaller changes lifted the power output by 25 percent to 300bhp at 5900rpm, and peak torque by 10 percent to 283.4lb ft at 4500rpm. Performance climbed several rungs up the supercar ladder, too. All the way to 155mph with 60mph coming up from rest in a very fit 6.2 seconds, 100mph in 14.8 seconds and 50-70mph in top in 7.3 seconds.

Here, then, was the muscle to exploit that exceptional chassis. I wrote *Motor*'s 1980 road test of the 928S and commented that 'the determined driver could use the extra power of the S to balance the car's attitude through a fast bend and, if conditions permit, power past the apex on a few degrees of easily held opposite lock.'

In 1984, it was the turn of 928S2 which, for the first time, offered ABS anti-lock brakes as an option and boasted the latest Bosch LH Jetronic fuel injection with overrun cut-off. Maximum power was 310bhp at 5900rpm backed up by 295lb ft of torque at 4100rpm. Top speed went up to 158mph and the 0-60mph time down to just under 6.5 seconds.

If it seemed that the opposition had the 928 firmly in its sights, the sleeker and better looking 1987 S4 with its smoother nose, new tail lights and prominent rear fender moved smartly out of range. A five-liter engine with four valves per cylinder driven by twin overhead camshafts atop each bank of cylinders and a 13 percent reduction in drag made the critical difference. Power went up a further 10bhp to 320bhp and torque an additional 22lb ft to 317lb ft. The top speed was a breathtaking 165mph and the 0-60mph time dropped to six seconds.

In the following year came the slightly hotter and mildly stripped out Club Sport version and, soon after that, for the

UK only, the Special Equipment – a Club Sport with luxury kit intact. The SE was a sort of dry run for the 928GT which went on sale in 1990 with a factory signed and sealed 330bhp and most of the SE's equipment, including a multi-function computer called the 'Porsche Information and Diagnostic System.' This continuously monitored all of the car's main systems, and even gave out a warning for low tire pressure.

Predictably, perhaps, Porsche saved the best for last. Billed by most observers as the final 928 before Porsche's much rumored four-seater, the 1992 GTS had the most of everything: a 5.4-liter version of the quad cam, 32-valve V8 pushing out a heavy-duty 350bhp at 5700rpm and 362lb ft of torque at 4250rpm; revised rear-end styling with still wider haunches; and new Carrera Turbo-style alloy wheels. I wrote the road test for *Autocar & Motor* and came away as impressed as when I tested the 928S all those years before. Barely faster than the GT from a standing start or in top speed, it had murderous fourth and fifth gear pulling power and despatched the fourth gear 50-70mph time in a stunning 3.7 seconds.

LEFT: The 928 GT will be remembered as one of the best – 170mph, storming acceleration, and amazing handling for such a bulky car.

ABOVE: The tailgate spoiler on this 928S4 is made from soft rubber.

CHAPTER 4

Towards 2000: After the 911

The thinking behind the 944 was to make the sportscar a real Porsche with a *real* Porsche engine. As a logical development of the 924 that was never going to be easy and, as things turned out, the brief was almost impossibly hard.

Conceived in 1977, the year the 928 was born, the 944's *raison d'etre* and chief selling hook was its engine. In simple terms, Porsche took a saw to the 928's alloy V8 and made itself a 2.5-liter slant four to go in a beefier yet still sleeker 924 with uprated suspension and fatter wheels and tires. In the event, it wasn't that straightforward, or anything like it. In fact, in the early stages, Porsche considered lopping off

two cylinders in the other plane to create a new V6 and, to that end, experimented with a Peugeot-Renault-Volvo V6.

In the end, though, four cylinders won the day. Not an orthodox four-pot big banger, mind you. With Mitsubishi-style twin balancer shafts – located at different heights on both sides of the cylinder block to balance the second-order vibrations common to all in-line four-cylinder engines – this engine could be made to spin much more smoothly than any conventional 'four.'

Consider also that merely chopping a 928 engine in half would have resulted in a single overhead cam four-cylinder unit of 2.25 liters – a bit small for Porsche's initial 160-200bhp target. Increasing the capacity to 2.5 liters by stretching the bore fixed that problem but gave very over-square bore/stroke dimensions of 100/78.9mm – good news for flexibility but less sanguine for economy. A longer stroke would have made the engine too tall. As it was it needed to be tilted over at 30 degrees to clear the hood line.

At least the fully electronic control for both ignition advance and fuel injection – Bosche Motronic breakerless ignition and Bosche L-Jetronic injection – kept a tight rein on the engine's potentially heavy thirst. Lusty it clearly was, developing 163bhp at 5800rpm and 151lb ft of torque at 3000rpm. This compared with 125bhp for the normally-aspirated two-liter 924 and 177 and 210bhp respectively for the 924 Turbo and Carrera GTS.

A strengthened version of the 924's five-speed transmis-

LEFT: The 944, a real Porsche based on the Audi-derived 924. It drew much of its character from its deep-chested 2.5-liter four-cylinder engine.

ABOVE: Styling changes centered around flared wheelarches.

RIGHT: The 944 engine span smoothly for a big-banger 'four' thanks to its contra-rotating balancer shafts.

LEFT: The 1989 944 Turbo toted a whopping 220bhp and enough performance to embarrass a 911.

BELOW: The Turbo was distinguished, visually, by a smoother nose treatment (BELOW LEFT); and (BELOW) special alloy wheels.

RIGHT: The 944S was the first 944 to get 16 valves.

OVERLEAF: The 1990 944 Cabriolet – even better looking than the coupe.

sion with slightly higher ratios (three-speed automatic was optional) took drive to the rear wheels, while the 944's chassis was based closely on that of the 924 Carrera GT. The new car used similar rack and pinion steering but settings for the strut front/semi-trailing arm rear suspension were revised. It also had stronger semi-trailing arms, meaty front and rear anti-roll bars and a 1.8in longer wheelbase. Braking was by ventilated disks all round.

The 944 also aped the Carrera GT's bulging arches, but without the deliberately 'tacked on' look; they were now an integral part of the galvanized steel body. With them went wider wheels and tires – 185/70VR 15 Pirelli CN36s on 7×15in with 215/60s as a cost option.

On the inside, the changes were less extreme but a 911-style three-spoke steering wheel and better grade trim material and carpeting helped the all important impression of quality. The motoring Press remained disappointed with the cabin, however, due to the poor instruments, dreary ambiance and low-wheeled driving position.

No moans about the way it went though. Porsche's 137mph claim was confirmed by numerous independent tests while reports of 0-60mph in around seven seconds and 0-100 mph in 20 were no less common. Yet even when driven hard, the 944 still managed to return around 25mpg.

Beautifully as the 924 handled, the 944 was better still, with a heady mixture of iron grip and terrific cornering balance, especially on the limit. The ride remained somewhat choppy but was never less than beautifully controlled. Within a year of its launch, the 944 had overshadowed the 924; the newcomer accounting for over half of total Porsche sales. But that wasn't the end of the story – far from it.

In 1983, in an effort to smarten up the 944's aesthetic act, its interior was re-trimmed in a much more elegant pinstripe fabric. A new design of alloy road wheel was also introduced. Much bigger changes, however, were scheduled for 1985 and the debut of the Turbo.

Right from the start, a turbocharged version of the 944 had been planned, just as it had been with the 924. An inkling of what might be in store came in 1981 when a 924 GTP driven by Walter Rohrl and Jurgen Barth finished 7th at Le Mans. Powered by a new turbocharged 2.5-liter in-line 'four,' it was a prototype racer for the road-going 944 Turbo.

For the first time, Porsche combined fully electronic ignition with a timed fuel-injection system, an alliance that gave reliability a big boost. As a basic goal, Porsche wanted the Turbo to develop the same power with a 'cat' as without – a brief it comfortably met – but improvements over the normally-aspirated 944 were far reaching.

They included a new combustion chamber with high turbulence and thermal efficiency. The design depended on a relatively high (8.0:1) compression ratio to maintain good off-boost torque and to guard against detonation. A knock sensor was part of the Bosch Motronic injection/ignition management system.

Water cooling for the KKK Type K26 turbocharger (maximum boost 11psi) and the use of an intercooler kept operating temperatures down. Peak power was increased by a whopping 35 percent to 220bhp at 5800rpm while, at 243lb ft, the turbo powerplant developed some 40lb ft more than the 911 Carrera's normally aspirated 3.2-liter flat six.

Motor magazine's test car posted 158mph and 0-60mph in 5.9 seconds – simply storming results – yet the road test

commented that 'in normal driving the 944 Turbo can be a sublimely docile machine, responsive yet velvet-gloved.'

To cope with the extra power, the 944's drivetrain was granted a bigger clutch with high-friction face material and a stronger five-speed transmission. Bodywork changes were mild: a new, smoother nose section, flush windshield, flared sills, a re-shaped tail spoiler, and a rear under-bumper aerofoil brought the Cd down from 0.35 to 0.33. There were plenty of changes under the skin, too, with four-piston fixed caliper brakes, cast aluminum suspension arms, re-rated spring and shock absorbers and 'phone-dial'-style cast aluminum wheels. Power steering became standard.

Could the chassis handle the extra power? I knew after a brief drive in the south of France where Porsche held the car's international launch, writing for *Motor*: 'There's understeer to be sure, but only to a degree that settles the car when entering a bend; it's never excessive. Grip is simply tremendous and matched with unflappable stability over bumps.'

Just two years after the Turbo's introduction, Porsche entered another phase of development with the twin-cam, 16-valve 944S which developed 188bhp. It would do in excess of 140mph and 0-60mph acceleration was seven seconds or a little less. It's career was a short one, though, because in 1989, the 944 range was squeezed down to two models: the Turbo (now with 250bhp) and the 944S2 powered by a three-liter version of the 16-valve engine delivering an extremely robust 211bhp.

Cosmetically, the S2 looked very similar to the Turbo and boasted much of its standard equipment which included ABS brakes with ventilated disks all round, and the wheels, tires and suspension/shock absorber settings of the original Turbo – essential considering the S2's prodigious performance: 146mph and 0-60mph in six seconds, according to *Autocar & Motor*.

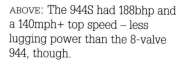

ABOVE: The 944S had 188bhp and a 140mph+ top speed – less lugging power than the 8-valve 944, though.

LEFT: The 968 engine introduced 'VariCam' variable valve timing, but no turbo version.

RIGHT: The 1990 944 Cabriolet.

A year later a Cabriolet version emerged with an electrically powered hood. It was perhaps, the prettiest 944 of all. The 924 was dropped in 1988 and, by this time, the 944 had done much to eradicate the 'posh Audi' image.

With the '80 percent new' 1991 968, however, Porsche believed it was back in business with the real deal. The 968 was a new car based on a fairly radical facelift of an old one. It had a 928-esque nose and tail treatment, a six-speed Getrag transmission as standard, the option of Porsche's brilliant Tiptronic automatic whole drive line, variable valve timing for the 16-valve big-banger 'four' to give class-leading torque, an up-rated chassis, bigger brakes, 911 Turbo style alloy wheels to cool them, and a host of cosmetic niceties. What's more it was built by Porsche in Zuffenhausen.

Its three-liter, 16-valve four-cylinder engine had the wick turned up still further to deliver 240bhp at 6200rpm and 225lb ft of torque at 4100rpm; the highest output of any naturally aspirated three-liter engine then in production. Porsche claimed a top speed of 156mph and a 0-60mph of 6.5 seconds for the six-speeder (not far off the old 944 Turbo's figures). 153mph and 7.9 seconds were the corresponding figures for the Tiptronic.

The 968 used the 944's suspension – wishbones, MacPherson struts and coils at the front, semi-trailing arms and transverse torsion bars at the rear, anti-roll bars at either end – but with spring and shock absorber settings revised to give the 968 the tautness and control of the old 944 Turbo.

'Cup' design 16in cast alloy road wheels wearing 205/55 and 225/50 ZR rated tires were standard, but they changed to 17in wheels of the same design fitted with 225/45 and 255/50 ZR tires, if the optional sports suspension was ordered with its adjustable shock absorbers, height-adjustable spring platforms, and still stiffer springs and shock absorbers. The sports suspension pack also included

larger front brakes, though, with ABS-backed ventilated disks and four-pot fixed calipers all round, the standard system was already formidable.

Even in the early '90s, the 968 made a strong case for itself: for the flexibility and responsiveness of its engine, the poise and balance of its chassis, the excellence of its build quality, and the sheer feeling of finely honed engineering the car exuded at all times. Taken together, these virtues are enough to keep the 968's nose in front of most, if not all, of the competition.

LEFT: The 968's styling sought to graft elements of the 928 on to the 944 – not altogether successfully in some people's view.

ABOVE RIGHT: Porsche's semi-automatic Tiptronic transmission was offered on the 968 but didn't work as well as it had on the Carrera 2/4.

RIGHT: As with the 944, there was a 968 Cabriolet.

LEFT: The 968 Cabrio shows different rear-end treatment – note the raised trunk.

BELOW: Lighter and more powerful, the 1992 968 Club Sport was designed to take on ever-more capable rivals, most notably Mazda's RX-7.

Index

Page numbers in *italics*
refer to illustrations

ABS anti-lock brakes 56,
    58, 66, 69
air conditioning 56, 58
Alfa Romeo Alfetta 43
Aston Martin V8 51, 56
Audi engine and parts 43,
    45
Austro-Daimler company 7
Autocar 46
Autocar and Motor 26, 31,
    59, 66

Barth, Jurgen 63
Berlin-Rome road race 8
Bodenkreditanstalt bank 7
brakes 11, 29, 31, 36, 40, 46
    ABS anti-lock 56, 58, 66,
        69
    all-wheel disks 8, 14, 52,
        63
    mechanically operated 8

Chassis 8, 14, 29, 41, 45, 52,
    63, 66, 69

Daimler Company 7
    250bhp SSKL 7
    Prince Henry model 7

Engines, for
    356, *6*, 8, 11
        1600C, 1600S, 1600SC,
            Super 90 14, *14-15*
    911 23, 26, *31*, 51
    924 61
    924 Carrera GTS 61
    924 Turbo 46, 61
    924S 51
    928 56, 58
    928GTS 59
        water-cooled V8 51, *51*,
            52, 59, 61
    944 51, 61
    968 69

Facia 11, 14, *15, 19, 38*, 46,
    56

Ferrari cars 56
    F40 38
    Testarossa 26
four-wheel drive 26, 31
Frankfurt Motor Show 23
fuel injection 63
    Bosche K-Jetronic 43, 46,
        52
    Bosche L-Jetronic 61
    Bosche LH-Jetronic 58

Gears 8, 11, 31
    fully automatic 26
    manual 26
Geneva Motor Show, 1977
    51
Gmund, Porsche company
    at 7, *8*

Handling 11, 14, 26, 29, 31,
    56, 63, 66
heating and ventilation 56,
    58
Hoffman, Max 8

Ignition systems 48, 63
    Bosche Motronic 61, 63
    Siemens-Hartig 48

Jaguar cars,
    XJ220 38
    XJS 51, 56

Komenda, Erwin 7, 8, 23

Lamborghini cars 52
Lapine, Tony 52
Le Mans races 21, 48
Lohner, Jacob 7

McLaren F1 cars 38
MacPherson struts 45, 46
Mazda RX-7 car 70
Miura cars 52
Motor 48, 58, 59, 63, 66
motor sport 7, 14, 21, 23

Peugeot company 23
Porsche, Professor
    Ferdinand *6*
    early years 7
    imprisonment by French
        7
    joins Daimler company 7
    joins Steyr Group 7
    own design business in
        Stuttgart 77
    sportscar interest 14
    and 356 model 11

Porsche, Ferdinand
    Alexander 'Butzi' *21*,
    23
Porsche, Ferdinand Piech
    23
Porsche, Ferry 7, 8
    and 356 7-8, *8*
    and 911 21, 23
Porsche, Dr Ing hc
    Ferdinand, GmbH 7,
    14, 26, 31, 35, 43, 51,
    59, 69
    move to Gmund 7
Porsche badge 8, 11
Porsche cars,
    356 *6*, 7-8
    1948 *8*
    1949 *9*
    1951 *10*
    1952 11
    1955 Speedster *11-15*,
        14
    1956 356A 14
    1959 Cabriolet Super
        90 14, *16-17*
    1960 356B 14
    1962 356B 14, *18*
    1963 356C 14
    Carrera model 8, 14
    911 14, *20-21*, 31, 46, 51,
        52
    911 Carrera 4 *2-3*
    911S 23, *24-5*
    1969 911E *22*
    1973 911 Carrera RS *4-5*,
        23, 35, *36-7*
        Carrera RSR *36*
    1975 911 Turbo-charged
        23, 26, *26*
    1978 911SC *23*, 26
    1982 911SC Carrera *23*,
        26, 31
    1987 911 Turbo Sport *29*
    1988 911 Carrera 4 26, 29,
        30-31, 38, 63
    1989 911 Carrera Cup
        model *32*
    1990 911 Carrera RS 31,
        35, 38, 40
        Cabrio model 23, 31,
        35
        Speedster 23, *29*
    1993 911 Carrera 2 RS 31,
        34-5, 36, 38, 40
    1976 924 43, 45-6, 51, 56,
        61, 63, 69
        Carrera GT *47*, 48, 63
        GTP 63
        Turbo model 46, *46*, 48

1985 924S 48, *49*, 51
1977 928, 2+2 GT 43,
    50-53, 51-2, 56, *56-7*,
    58, 69
1980 928S *54-5*, 56, *57*,
    58, 59
1984 928S2 58
1987 928S4 *57*, 58
1988 928 Club Sport 58-9
1990 928GT *58-9*, 59
1992 928GTS 59
935/78 racers 23
    'Moby Dick' 23
944 46, 51, *60-61*, 61, 63,
    69
    1983 model 63
1985 944 Turbo *62*, 63, 66
1987 944S *63*, 66, *66*
1989 944S2 66
1990 944 Cabriolet *64-5*,
    67, 69
1988 959 *1*, 21, *38, 40*
    1984 design study for
    41
1991 968 *66*, *68-9*, 69
    968 Cabriolet *69-70*
1992 968 Club Sport *70*
Porsche Information and
    Diagnostic System
    59
production volume 7-8, 11,
    14

Rabe, Karl 7, 8
Reutter Karosserie
    coachworks 8, *8*
rev-counter 11, *18*
Rohrl, Walter 63
Rosenberger, Adolf 7

Shock absorbers 11, 66
Siemens-Hartig digital
    ignition system 48
Solex carburetors 8
soundproofing 11
speed 8, 11, 26, 35, 46, 48,
    51, 56, 58, 59, 63, 66
steering 56, 58, 63, 66
    see also handling
Steyr group 7
styling 8, 14, *16-18*, 23, 26,
    26, 29-31, 41, 46, 52,
    60, 66
    by 'Butzi' Porsche *21*, 23
    by Komenda 8
    by Lapine 52, *52-3*
    'tulip form' shape 7
suspension 8, 11, 43, 5
45-6, 66, 69

Tiptronic whole drive line 26, 29, 31, 69
tires 14, 23, 36, 48, 56, 58, 63, 66, 69
Tomala, Hans 23
transaxle layout 43, 45, 51
transmission 26, 61, 63
 five-speed 35, 46, 52, 66

Getrag 69
synchromesh 11
three-speed auto 52, 63
turbocharger, KKK 46, 48, 63

United States safety regulations 23

Volkswagen company 43 181 45
 Beetle 7, 8, 21, 46
 Golf 45
 Scirocco 45

Weights 35, 52
Weissach rear axle 56

wheels 14, 23, 36, *49*, 52, *52*, 58, 59, *62*, 63, 66, 69

Zolder track 31, 35, 38, 40
Zuffenhausen works *6, 8*, 26, 46, 69

ACKNOWLEDGMENTS

The author and publisher would like to thank Stephen Small for editing this book, David Eldred for his design work and Ron Watson for compiling the index. The following individuals and agencies provided photographic material:

Brompton Books, pages: 6-7(all three), 8(both), 21(top), 26(top/Nicky Wright).

Neill Bruce, pages: 1(courtesy of Dick Lovett Ltd), 2-3, 10-11(all four), 12-13, 19, 20, 21(bottom), 23(top), 24-25, 26(center), 27(The Peter Roberts Collection), 29(The Midland Motor Museum, Bridgnorth), 30-31(all four), 36-37(all three, bottom left/The Midland Motor Museum, Bridgnorth), 38(top), 39(top/ courtesy of Dick Lovett Ltd), 39(bottom), 40(both), 44-45(all three/The Midland Motor Museum, Bridgnorth), 50(The Nigel Dawes Collection), 52(top/The Nigel Dawes Collection), 52(bottom), 54-55(The Nigel Dawes Collection).

Colin Burnham, pages: 14-15(all four), 18(bottom).

Andrew Morland, pages: 26(bottom), 41(both), 42(bottom), 47(top), 61(bottom), 63, 66(top), 68-69(all three), 70(top).

Don Morley, page: 22(both).

National Motor Museum, England, pages: 4-5, 9(both), 16-17, 18(top/Nicky Wright), 27(bottom/Nicky Wright), 28(top), 42(top), 46(Nicky Wright), 48-49(both), 51, 53(both), 56-57(all four), 58-59(both), 60(Nicky Wright), 61(top), 62(all three), 64-65, 67.

Porsche, pages: 38(bottom), 43, 66(bottom).

TRH, pages: 28(bottom), 32-33(all three), 34-35(both), 47(bottom), 70(bottom).